Why shouldnt Israel exist in the Middle East?

AF064196

A

Hans Jansen

Why shouldnt Israel exist in the Middle East?

A Synopsis

Aspekt Publishers

Why schouldnt Israel exist in the Middle East?
A Synopsis
© Hans Jansen
© 2017 Aspekt Publishers
Amersfoortsestraat 27, 3769 AD Soesterberg, Nederland
info@uitgeverijaspekt.nl-http://www.uitgeverijaspekt.nl

Cover design: Maarten Bakker
Interior: Mariska Rooth

ISBN: 9789463382298
NUR: 400

All rights reserved. No reproduction copy or transmission of this publication may be made without written permission.

CONTENTS

Reading guide Breaking through the indifference   7

Preface
Is peace possible if one side wants to murder the other?   11
(Benno Barnard)

Part 1
That Israel has no right to exist is a widespread belief in   21
the Middle East

1 No place for the Jewish State   23
2 Arab leaders meet in Bloudan   26
3 Four times 'no'   31
4 Not changed one iota   33
5 Bloudan endorsed by academics   37
6 It starts with textbooks   39
7 The imam's sermon   42
8 A colonial question   45

Part 2
Why does Israel not have the right to exist in the Middle East?   47

1 Humiliated by the victorious Jew   51
2 Holy ground   57
3 The cult of death   61

Reading guide

BREAKING THROUGH THE INDIFFERENCE

My book *Why shouldn't Israel exist in the Middle East?* first appeared in 2015. While writing the book, I kept asking myself the question: how can we explain the deafening silence of the world's media about the deep-seated conviction of the majority of political and religious leaders in the Middle East that the State of Israel does not even have a right to exist? Why are there any hardly protests in the European Parliament or in the Dutch House of Representatives? Consider, meanwhile, that Mahmoud Abbas was received with great honour by the entire cabinet in autumn 2015. I once asked Elie Wiesel, my greatest mentor, how this silence could be explained. The answer he gave speaks volumes: "The world is silent because people are indifferent. This indifference is the great danger, and the Jews have always been its first victims!"

Indeed, the genocide of six million Jews could not have happened solely as a result of an ideology of hatred and enmity, but also because of a profound indifference. Elie Wiesel spent his whole life warning of the dangers of this indifference. In May 1988, as a survivor of Auschwitz, author of many novels and stories, professor of literature and philosophy and winner of the Nobel Peace Prize, he opened the international exhibition *Anti-Semitism: a history in words and images* at the Anne Frank House in Amsterdam. In his magisterial speech he said: "Anti-Semitism is bad not only for the victim, but also for the bystander. There were three roles in the tragedy of the Second World War: the murderer, the victim and the bystander. And without the bystander, the murderer could never have victimised so many people. All my life I have tried to fight the indifference of the bystander. Because the Jews, throughout the age-old history of anti-Semitism and even now in our own time, have always been the first victims of this indifference.

I have always believed that the opposite of love is not hate, but indifference. And that means that the opposite of knowledge is not ignorance, but indifference. The opposite of hope is not living without hope, but living with indifference. The opposite of life is not death, but indifference to life and death. And for this reason I believe that literature or art or writing, or teaching or working for the good of humanity all have one ultimate goal: to fight against indifference (…). Indifference undermines everything, it lulls people to sleep and robs them of life even before actually killing. Indifference is the most insidious of all dangers."

Indifference is a recurring theme in Elie Wiesel's many speeches, interviews and studies. He came back to it once again in his speech in Oslo on 11 December 1986, when he was presented with the Nobel Peace Prize: "Israel is the only nation in the world whose very existence is threatened. (…) Action is the only remedy to indifference, the most insidious danger of all. (…) There is so much to be done, there is so much that can be done. One person – an Albert Schweitzer, a Raoul Wallenberg, a Martin Luther King, a Mahatma Gandhi – one person of integrity and courage, can make a difference, a difference of life and death."

In his book Erasmus and the Jews (Chicago 1986), the renowned Russian scholar Shimon Markish comes to the remarkable conclusion that Desiderius Erasmus was not an anti-Semite, nor a philo-Semite, but rather an a-Semite. He proved again and again in his life that he was utterly indifferent to the fate of the Jews who were threatened with death. I really do not know how many anti-Semites live here in the Netherlands, nor indeed how many philo-Semites there are, but I am very afraid that in our country (and elsewhere) the number of a-Semites has become alarmingly high.

Spiritual and political leaders cannot remain indifferent. Indifference undermines everything, as I said. It lulls people to sleep even before it kills. Indifference is the most insidious of all dangers, because in our world there are few people who are prepared not to be bystanders. We must break through indifference. Make no mistake about it: indifference in the face of evil means acquiescence in evil itself, complicity in evil!

That is why I wrote the book: *Why shouldn't Israel exist in the Middle East?*, of which you are now reading a synopsis. This book is intended as an accessible introduction, intended for a wide audience. I shall therefore confine myself to the broad outlines and for notes and appendices I shall refer as far as possible to the original book.

Preface

IS PEACE POSSIBLE IF ONE SIDE WANTS TO MURDER THE OTHER?

Hans Jansen has written an overwhelming book – literally, because it is over a thousand pages long and you can use it to strike an enemy dead, like the jaw-bone of an ass... It's called: *Why shouldn't Israel exist in the Middle East?* and that is an excellent question. A double question even why Israel allowed the Muslim states do not exist, but also why the part of Western elites may not exist?

First something about the second question. As you know, there is, also here in Belgium and the Netherlands, an irrational hatred of Israel. It is my belief that this hatred is based on anti-Semitism, perhaps not a conscious anti-Semitism, but an atavistic anti-Semitism that exists throughout the Christian world and which can become active in every individual at any time via the collective subconscious. That unconscious racism prepares the minds of an embarrassingly large number of intellectuals for the activation of all the pulleys in their fully automated thinking.

I was reminded of this phenomenon when I recently visited the Israeli Embassy in Brussels. That embassy is, of necessity, a fort, located in a secluded side street full of concrete blocks, guarded by paratroopers cradling their machine-guns like a baby, and the building itself is surrounded by a security wall, fitted with dozens of cyclopic eyes. But, once you get inside, everyone smiles at you, says shalom and cracks jokes. And so it is a metaphor for Israel itself.

I had to think back to the Six-Day War of 1967. Again I saw my parents sitting by the radio (we had no television), and again I saw my father's raised fist when he exclaimed, "Damn, damn, they've driven them into the desert!" Tears ran down his cheeks; for him, it was if a new Germany had been defeated.

After 1967, and especially after the Yom Kippur War of 1973, the sympathy that existed in the Netherlands for Israel gradually ebbed away. I'm not going to delve too deeply into that development – but the fact is that there is a powerful pro-Palestinian lobby, supported by the brains and big mouths of many left-wing intellectuals and the even bigger mouths of many Muslims living here.

A few examples. The Catholic former Dutch Prime Minister Dries van Agt has shouted from every available rooftop about how bad Israel is and about how we need to talk urgently with those nice, reasonable people of Hamas.

On the VRT I heard him state that in 1948 'millions' of Palestinians were expelled. In The Hague, twenty or so burka-clad people were demonstrating in favour of that most abused of words: freedom. One of the people present scolded a journalist. He called him 'Jew dog'.

And the Belgian 'Poet Laureate' Charles Ducal certainly does not want the Jews to have their own country and published a shocking anti-Semitic poem (I wrote about it in *Joods Actueel*).

To all these people I say: 'Are you against Israel? Fine, but we cannot be friends, even though you are certainly intelligent enough to camouflage your anti-Semitism as anti-Zionism and stupid enough not to recognise itself as no more Jew-hatred.'

Anti-Semitism is the elusive substance into which Evil has retreated – it is the devil who cannot keep his mouth shut. But because the devil is very cunning, he has now hidden in the oh so misleading term 'anti-Zionism'. European decadence consists of the fact that the majority of the European intelligentsia do not want to understand that 'the Palestinian issue' is not about land, but is a pan-Arab and pan-Islamic project to destroy Israel. The easiest way you can demonstrate that is with images from a large country which has a peace accord with Israel, namely Egypt.

During the Gaza war of 2014, there were Egyptians demonstrating outside the Israeli embassy in Cairo. On their placards were swastikas and words such as 'The Gas Chambers Are Ready'. People like Dries van Agt and Lucas Catherine and their sympathisers are committing a crime by remaining silent about this.

These placards illustrate what Hans Jansen proves in his book: that Israel is surrounded by Jew hatred. I cite page 597: 'Depicting Zionists and Jews as "descendants of apes and pigs", which worldwide is a traditional theme in Islam (in the Koran, the Hadith, the exegesis of the Koran and the sermons of imams), but which in the past was of no practical significance for their dealings with Jews, very widespread only became relevant after the Six-Day War and in recent years in the media in the Arab and Muslim world, as a result of the Second Intifada.'

During the last Gaza war, the members of the leftist mosque vomited the usual ritual curses, that satisfied a deep anti-Semitism. Israel – always in response to aggression – only attacked military targets, while Hamas systematically targeted civilians… ah, how convenient it is to forget this. I tried to have a conversation with some of them about the true nature of Hamas. That conversation was impossible. The poor Palestinians lived in wretched conditions. The West treated them very badly. The Jews practiced apartheid, genocide and any number of reprehensible things. The European Union should immediately boycott Israel. This last demand is simply the modern version of what the Sturmabteilung and vindictive bourgeois Germans chalked on Jewish shop windows in the thirties: *Kauft nicht bei Juden!*

Why do highly educated leftists not want to understand the true nature of Hamas? What explains the monstrous covenant between European Communists/Socialists and bloodthirsty, misogynistic maniacs with a medieval worldview?

I think I know the answer. Hamas (and the whole Islamic world) poses, with a certain dramatic flair, as the victim, and the left has always been fond of victims. Moreover, Hamas also cherishes a utopia. And utopians recognise others of the same species, like dogs. In the utopia of Hamas, the world is a place that has been purified of Jews – and in order to achieve this paradisiacal state, it is, for example, desirable to murder Jewish toddlers, because otherwise they will grow up to become soldiers of the Zionist Entity. This isn't some sick joke, it really is part of Hamas's battle plan. Meanwhile, Palestinian children from the Gaza Strip are receiving free treatment in Israeli hospitals.

In the Islamic fundamentalist utopia, therefore, everything begins with the extermination of the Jews. Western utopians are very careful to keep quiet about this bothersome aspect of the Palestinian dream. Applauding it would cause them too much embarrassment, even though I think some of them would privately believe that the Jews had brought their own doom on themselves – this latter point being entirely within the tradition of great European anti-Semites, such as the Comte de Gobineau and H.S. Chamberlain.

There is also this aspect: the possibility of accusing the Jews themselves of 'acting like Nazis' and organising a 'Palestinian Holocaust' (because they read all those shocking allegations) relieves the good people of the left from that nagging, unbearable guilt about our anti-Semitic European past.

But it is in fact much worse than this. The biggest shock Hans Jansen has for us in his book is that the extremist vision of Hamas, Iran, Hezbollah, the suicide bombers... is that of an overwhelming majority of Muslims. That starts with education: each new generation will hate the Jews as enthusiastically as the last one. By way of illustration, I give you the chapter titles in Professor Jansen's book concerning education in the Middle East:

- Education by the Israeli government in the service of peaceful coexistence between Palestinians and Israelis
- Education by the authorities in Syria encourages students to destroy Israel in holy war
- Education by the authorities in Saudi Arabia encourages students to destroy Israel in jihad
- Education by the authorities in Egypt encourages students to destroy Israel in jihad

- Education in the Iranian Islamic Republic encourages students to destroy Israel in jihad

Am I an enemy of Islam? Is Hans Jansen?

Well, I will let a real enemy of Islam say a few words. This is a commentary on Hamas: 'For Muslims, killing is a leisure activity. And if they can't find an enemy to kill, they will kill one another. It is impossible that a people who bring up their children with ideas of death and martyrdom – and this in order to please the Creator – can simultaneously teach a love of life.'

These are the words of an Arab woman, Wafa Sultan, a Syrian sociologist working in the United States.

The dangers that threaten Israel are dangers facing the entire Western world. Islam has enough fundamentalists to keep us engaged in a protracted war. And Israel is the ideological frontline, even when there is no de facto fighting. Islamic fundamentalism is our common enemy. But it is difficult for us, the Europeans of today, to recognise an enemy when we see one. Our civilisation has been undermined not just by ecophobia – the aversion to one's own civilisation born from vague feelings of unease – but also by psychology. Thanks to psychology, you can point an accusing finger at your parents, but not at an enemy. Enemies are people who themselves have been deformed by their parents and are therefore not to blame.

Am I exaggerating?

In 2010, when I physically encountered the intolerance of Islam –Sharia Belgium prevented me from giving a lecture at the University of Antwerp – the leftist press taunted me, saying I had brought it on myself. It now turns out that I was more right than even I had feared at the time: the members of Sharia Belgium are in prison or have joined IS. One of the guys who stood in front of me then is now head of the religious police in Raqqa and is throwing gay people from rooftops. And as evidence of Islamic intolerance, we need here, today, in a Western European city, in 2015, heavily armed paratroopers outside our door.

But it is not only jihadis who are our enemies, so are all the other Jew-haters and condemners of Israel, from Lucas Catherine to Abou Jahjah. When Bart De Wever called for the army to protect Jewish institutions, Abou Jahjah tweeted, in appalling Dutch: 'Where was your army when Hans Van Themsche shot down immigrants and children in broad daylight in Antwerp?' The tweet was sent for the attention of 'Zionist fellator'. I do not think we can deduce from this that De Wever sometimes performed the aforementioned sexual act with Zionists – rather that, in the eyes of Abou Jahjah, anyone who wants to protect the Jewish community is a Zionist. Which means that the members of the Jewish community must then, a fortiori, be Zionists, in other words: bad people you can shoot with a clear conscience.

On page 847 of his book, Hans Jansen quotes Al Jazeera, a channel that most Westerners believe represents Arab decency. 'A certain talk show was discussing this interesting question: Is Zionism worse than Nazism? During the debate Dr Faisal al-Qassem, the moderator, read out the opinion of a viewer who had e-mailed: "The sons of Zion, whom our God characterised as the sons of apes and pigs, will not be repelled until a new holocaust takes place (in the Middle East), which will destroy all the Jews at once, together with our traitors (those who now collaborate with them, the scum of the Islamic nation)." Thus, even in the entertainment industry, a virulent hatred of Israel is fostered in the countries that surround it.'

What exactly is a Zionist anyway? A Jew who has decided to fight back for the first time in 2000 years?

Back to anti-Zionism in the West. If you are against Israel, you are against the Jews, even if you don't know it yourself. The alliance on our streets during the last Gaza war with Muslims shouting 'all Jews to the gas chambers' is obviously inconvenient for left-wing intellectuals. To resolve that problem they employ the Semitic-semantic method: they declare that they are not anti-Semitic, but merely anti-Zionist. That gives them, in their own eyes at least, the right to spout all kinds of clichés about Israel – a terrorist state, after all, where hands are chopped off, women stoned and where you get forty lashes if you're caught with a glass of wine; the country that also hanged a nice, efficient man like Adolf Eichmann, even though he had done nothing more than what many extremists in the Middle East would be only too happy to do themselves…

I will give you one shocking quote (in the book you will find hundreds and hundreds) that Hans Jansen offers us on page 149: 'On 24 April 1961 the *Jerusalem Times* (an English-language newspaper in Jordan) published an open letter to Eichmann. This letter warmly congratulated Eichmann, as the organiser of the genocide of six million Jews in Europe, because by the destruction of the European Jews he had performed a great service for all mankind. This letter concludes as follows: "Of this I am sure: one day the Eichmann trial in Jerusalem will be decided by the liquidation of the remaining six million Jews."

Abdullah al-Tal, a member of the Jordanian Senate, characterised Eichmann as a martyr and protested against the way in which the Jews had dragged Hitler and the Nazis through the mud. He said, among other things: "Hitler did to the Jews what people had done with them for many generations in the past: they were killed, burned and expelled from countries in which they had betrayed and deceived people."'

During the last Gaza war there was a video on YouTube in which Hamas called on Palestinians to embrace death and form a human shield. The slain Hamas leader Nizar Rayan sent one of his own sons on a suicide mission (he had sons to spare, given that he had four wives). How can Israel and the West possibly ever come to any reasonable compromise with this sort of worldview? How can you make peace between two parties, if one of them wants to murder the other?

Meanwhile, Israel's small number of apologists always get the settlement thrown in their face. On the question of land, there is something very pertinent on page 858 of Hans Jansen's book: '(...) not just according to Hamas and other terrorist organisations, but also according to the Palestinian Authority, the Israeli-Palestinian conflict is not primarily a border conflict, but rather an irreconcilable religious war. Palestinian religious and academic leaders openly teach that the Israeli-Palestinian conflict is part of the irreconcilable war between Islam and the Jews. To justify this position, Palestinians incessantly cite Islamic sources, according to which it is a matter of religious dogma to hate Jews, and even the murdering of Jews is the will of Allah.'

Now would be a good time to again repeat the famous words of Golda Meir, from her autobiography *My Life* (1974): 'I have never doubted for an instant that the true aim of the

Arab states has always been, and still is, the total destruction of the State of Israel, or that even if we had gone back far beyond the 1967 lines to some miniature enclave, they would not still have tried to eradicate it and us.'

I congratulate Hans Jansen on his historical book. It is a masterpiece, which contains an almost unbearable weight of evidence regarding the Muslim hatred of Jews and Israel. Half of it consists of source material, quotes that conclusively prove what all these left-wing activists do not want to know.

This chapter is the text of the speech that Benno Barnard gave on 1 March 2015 at the presentation of the book *Why shouldn't Israel exist in the Middle East?*

Barnard is a poet and essayist who has been living in the UK since the end of 2015. Before that, he had lived in Belgium for many years.

1

That Israel has no right to exist is a widespread belief in the Middle East

1

NO PLACE FOR THE JEWISH STATE

On 26 October 2005, Mahmoud Ahmadinejad, the President of Iran, said: 'The State of Israel should not only destroyed, but will certainly be wiped off the map.' Ahmadinejad made this statement at a conference entitled 'The World without Zionism'. He referred to the former Iranian leader, Ayatollah Khomeini, who since 1989 had regularly called for the destruction of Israel. Ahmadinejad called Israel's existence 'a defeat and humiliation for the whole Islamic world', and added that nowhere in the new Middle East should there be a place for Israel. According to the new president of Iran, all the countries of the Middle East should be ethnically cleansed of Jews as soon as possible. On 30 August 2011, the leader of the Muslim Brotherhood in Egypt, Essam el-Erian, said in this regard: 'There can be no place for the Jewish state, either in the Arab world or anywhere else on planet Earth!'

There are countless politicians in Iran who agree with Ahmadinejad and seriously believe that Israel has no right to exist and should disappear from the earth. Between 2005 and 2012, when the President was in power in Tehran, he fulminated against his archenemies in Israel, in both short and very long speeches (often tirades!), even at meetings of the UN. In every possible way he wanted to explain that he could not tolerate that in 1948 an insignificant tiny Jewish state (in his eyes) had been born in the immensely great Arab world. He considered himself to be the mouthpiece of influential ayatollahs, imams, government leaders and members of the Revolutionary Guard. Without exaggeration we can say that his speeches reflected the official position of the big cheeses, the ruling authorities. The majority of all political and religious leaders in Iran, for whom Ayatollah Khomeini still has great authority, openly express the opinion that Israel has no right to exist anywhere in the Middle East and must therefore disappear.

In recent years Israeli governments have been protesting continuously at Ahmadinejad's tirades about seriously defying the right to existence of this small state in the Middle East. But in contrast to the successive governments of Israel, the entire Middle East (Egypt, Jordan, Syria, Saudi Arabia, Lebanon, Qatar, etc.) maintained a deafening silence on the outbursts of hate from the Iranian President, and those of his predecessors (Ayatollah Khomeini, Ayatollah Khamenei, Mohammad Khatami and Ayatollah Akbar). As far as I can see, and based on serious information from insiders in Israel, I regret to say that in the aforementioned countries of the Arab world not a single Sunni political or religious leader has to date condemned the often virulent anti-Semitic statements made by Ahmadinejad.

Is not that very strange? Why was the entire Arab world silent in the past seven years (2005-2012) when Ahmadinejad so often railed against Israel and demonised the Jewish nation in the most horrible way? Ahmadinejad himself will not have found it strange that political and religious leaders in the Middle East (all Sunnis!) did not voice any criticism of his very extensive diatribes against the Jewish nation. This is because the views that Ahmadinejad expressed had been widespread for a number of decades earlier in almost every country in the Middle East. Political and religious leaders in these countries had many years earlier become very familiar with the idea that the Jewish National Home (1917) and the State of Israel (1948) have no right to exist and must therefore be wiped off the map.

In his speeches, Ahmadinejad often neatly voiced the prevailing view of academics, professors, teachers, politicians, imams, jurists, journalists, columnists, cartoonists and creators of radio and television programs in the Middle East, that the small Jewish nation has no right to exist and must therefore be destroyed. It is an extremely naive misunderstanding on the part of European and American politicians to think that only terrorist groups such as Hezbollah and Hamas have this aim in view. The evidence for this is presented in detail in my book *Why shouldn't Israel exist in the Middle East?*

I devoted over twenty sections of my book to demonstrating that other Arab leaders consider that Israel should disappear from the earth as soon as possible, because this state has no right to exist. In recent decades, political and religious leaders in the European Union and the United States have not taken seriously the idea that a very large majority of Muslims in the Arab world have continued to believe (almost like a dogma) that the whole of Palestine is actually an Arab country and that it must ultimately become so again (Bernard Lewis). Paul Bogdanor wrote a shocking and heartbreaking article about this. Anyone who cares about the Israeli-Palestinian conflict should read it. It can be found in Appendix 3 of *Why shouldn't Israel exist in the Middle East?* Right up to the present day, European parliamentarians and American Congressmen have maintained a deafening silence about this, with all the fatal consequences.

2

ARAB LEADERS MEET IN BLOUDAN

Ahmadinejad's vision was nothing new. These ideas have been widespread since 1937. Even though Israel did not yet exist, the Jewish National Home was established in Palestine in 1917; in some Jewish circles in London, and above all in the countries of the Middle East, this was seen as being a miniature state. In several Arab countries it was openly declared that the Jewish National Home was in any case the beginning of a Jewish state in a predominantly Arab land. Leading politicians in Palestine, Egypt, Syria and Lebanon were fully convinced that this Jewish National Home could definitely claim no right to exist and therefore had to be destroyed unconditionally.

What had happened in Palestine? In 1937 the British government's Peel Commission decided to divide Palestine into two states: a small state for Jews and a big one for the Palestinians. Haj Amin al-Husseini, Grand Mufti of Jerusalem and an outspoken Jew-hater, was a fierce opponent of this decision. He considered it necessary that as many countries as possible from the Arab world should be approached to issue a powerful pan-Arab protest against the division of the country. He suggested convening a conference of leading politicians from different countries to discuss the division in detail. In Damascus, the Grand Mufti spoke to Anji al-Suwaidi (Iraq), Muhammad 'Ali Alluba Pasha (Egypt), Abdallah al-Yafi (Lebanon) and Lutfi al-Haffar (Syria). All four were of the opinion that the best place to hold such a conference would be Bloudan in Syria. But they also stressed that a large assembly would only make sense if the best politicians were invited. This would make it clear to everyone in the Middle East that the whole of Palestine was Arab and should undoubtedly remain Arab. Amin al-Husseini agreed to the proposal. The decision was taken to hold a pan-Arab conference at the Grand Hotel in Bloudan, Syria on 8, 9 and 10 September 1937 for up to five hundred delegates.

Finally, the Grand Mufti of Jerusalem explained once again that in their discussions at the conference the delegates should decide the following:

- The Jewish National Home must be wiped off the map.
- The division of Palestine into two states must be unconditionally rejected.
- Palestine must remain Arab for all eternity.

According to Husseini, after the scheduled three days the discussions in Bloudan could be rounded off with the decision to form an Arab government in the whole of Palestine.

The turnout for the Pan-Arab Conference in Bloudan exceeded all expectations, as 411 members from seven countries attended the opening on 8 September, including 160 Syrians and 128 Palestinians. As agreed, it was mainly politicians who put themselves forward to take part in the discussions of the political and economic committee. Fortunately, Sir Gilbert Mackereth, the British consul in Damascus, was prepared to write a detailed report of the Pan-Arab Conference. On 15 September 1937 he sent a voluminous report to the British government in London. The report was divided into a memorandum (an evaluation of the Conference), a comprehensive report (Proceedings of three committees), an essay on Jews and Muslims (compiled by Husseini) and a report on a secret meeting in Damascus, which took place after the Conference in Bloudan, on how to conduct of the jihad in Palestine against the Jewish National Home.

The political committee, consisting of Syrian, Lebanese, Palestinian, Egyptian, Iraqi and Trans-Jordanian politicians, adopted the following resolutions on 9 September 1937, which were then ratified by all 411 members of the Bloudan Conference:

- Palestine is an integral part of the Arab lands.
- Palestine must never be divided and the Jewish National Home should not be transformed into a state; a very strong position must be taken against these developments.
- The Balfour Declaration must be wiped off the map and Palestine should be declared to be no longer a mandated territory; the Arabs should conclude a treaty with the British based on the Iraqi model.
- The immigration of Jews should be irrevocably halted, and land may only be sold to Arabs, in accordance with the law.

The resolutions of the Conference were sent to the League of Nations and also to the governments of the aforementioned countries throughout the Middle East.

In the memorandum (evaluation of the Conference) the following resolutions were unanimously adopted by all the politicians in the Hotel Bloudan on 10 September 1937:

1. *The division of Palestine into two states is contrary to the rights of the Arabs, because they own the whole country.*
2. *Palestine is a part of the Arab/Islamic territory.*
3. *Palestine is a sacred part of the whole Islamic territory.*
4. *Palestine is a single, complete entity, from which nothing is missing and which is owned by the Arabs.*
5. *Every part of Palestine is the property of the great Arab nation.*
6. *Palestine is the inalienable property of the great Arab National Home.*
7. *The Palestinian problem in the country is the whole Islamic nation. It is the duty of all Arabs and Muslims to fight as one man anywhere in the world for the freedom and unity of Palestine, to prevent the creation of a Jewish state that will conquer the whole Middle East and will exploit Arabs everywhere.*
8. *The whole Arab Nation is urged to conduct a holy war (jihad) against the Jewish National Home.*

Haj Amin al-Husseini was strongly inspired in this respect by the founder of the Muslim Brotherhood, Hasan al-Banna, who wrote: 'Islam is the universal truth and Muslims have no loyalty other than to Islam. The purpose of jihad is to raise the banner of Islam. The sons of the Islamic nation (of which Palestine is a sacred part) must give their blood and lives for their country, until it encompasses the entire world. Participation in jihad is a duty for believers. It means slaughtering the infidels, plundering their wealth, destroying their shrines and smashing their idols.'

The many hundreds of bulletins of the Palestinian Authority, which I have received in recent years from Itamar Marcus and Nan Jacques Zilberdik in an English translation, have supplied me with almost weekly proof that the vision of

Bloudan is as current today as it has ever been. It is passed from one generation to the next. An example of this is the newsletter written by Tawfiq Tirawi, a member of the Fatah Central Committee, on 5 August 2014. As a leader of the Fatah party, he calls upon his readers to destroy Israel, 'Expel the occupiers from all the pure land that runs from the river to the sea.' For decades, I have read endless variations of what Tawfiq Tirawi is writing here about his own Fatah party. What he says about Palestine is very widespread throughout the countries of the Middle East.

3
FOUR TIMES 'NO'

From the war of independence (1947-1948) onwards, the policy of the Arab leaders in the Middle East was aimed at the destruction of the State of Israel, because all the political leaders shared the most profound conviction that Israel had no right to exist. The war was started by the Arabs, who refused to accept the UN resolution arranging the partition of Palestine into a Palestinian and a Jewish state and who wanted to destroy Israel. On 14 May 1948 Azzam Pasha, secretary general of the Arab League, said in Cairo: 'This will be a war of extermination and mass destruction, which will be spoken of in the same vein as the Mongolian massacres and the Crusades.' Six thousand Israelis were killed in this war of annihilation.

From the establishment of the State of Israel in 1948, the search for peace has been a permanent part of the policy of every Israeli government. The politics of the Arab states is diametrically opposite to that of Israel; they could not reconcile themselves to the existence of Israel and refused to recognise Israel. They did not give up their goal of destroying Israel, even if they admitted on occasion that it was not in their power to achieve this. On a military level, they pursued a policy of strengthening their military potential in order to be able to implement their work towards the destruction of Israel. Politically they tried to isolate Israel within the family of nations, and economically they followed a policy of boycott against

Israel. The propaganda of the Arab states was aimed at cultivating hatred and enmity towards Israel, distorting Israel's image by means of anti-Semitic stereotypes and by educating the young generation to take part in a struggle whose goal is to destroy Israel. At the borders, the Arab states followed a policy of exhaustion by means of terrorist acts, with the intention of disrupting normal life in Israel, and at sea Egypt tried to implement a blockade of Israel. It closed the Suez Canal to all Israeli shipping and the Straits of Tiran, at the entrance to the Gulf of Eilat, to all shipping to and from Israel.

Between 1957 and 1967 the process of Arab hostility and hatred did not weaken for one moment. Egypt remained the most important instrument of this, and this hatred was always openly expressed in the speeches and letters of the Egyptian president. Here are just four examples: (1) In a letter to King Hussein dated 13 March 1961, he wrote concerning Israel: 'We believe that the evil that was placed in the heart of the Arab world should be eradicated.' (2) In a radio speech made in Cairo on 24 February 1964, Nasser said: 'Everything points to war with Israel. We are the ones who will set the time, we are the ones who will set the place.' (3) On 25 May 1965 Nasser issued a joint statement with President Aref of Iraq: 'The Arab national effort is aimed at the elimination of Israel.' (4) On 23 July 1967 Nasser said: 'Life will have no meaning for us any more and will be worthless, if every square foot of the land of Palestine is not liberated.' No wonder that at the summit of Arab leaders that was held in Khartoum in August 1967, the infamous four 'no's' echoed from the mouths of all the Arab politicians and were recorded almost like dogma in the summit's minutes: no peace with Israel, no negotiations with Israel, no recognition of the State of Israel, and an insistence on the rights of the Palestinian people to their own country, namely the whole of Palestine.

4

NOT CHANGED ONE IOTA

The Charter of the Palestine Liberation Organization (PLO), which dates from 1968 (1-17 July), states even today in crystal-clear terms that Israel has no right to exist and therefore must be destroyed. The brilliant historian Benny Morris has proven clearly and unequivocally that the Constitution of the PLO has never been withdrawn or amended. 'The PLO has not changed one iota in its political program (...). The PLO works in phases. Allah willing, we shall drive them out of all of Palestine.' Palestinian leaders persist in their refusal to accept the Jewish nature of Israel. Below are the most important extracts from the resolutions of the Charter, which Mahmoud Abbas constantly invokes with reference to the Palestinian Authority when he speaks Arabic.

Article 1: Palestine is the homeland of the Arab Palestinian people; it is an indivisible part of the Arab homeland, and the Palestinian people are an integral part of the Arab nation.

Article 2: Palestine, with the boundaries it had during the British Mandate, is an indivisible territorial unit.

Article 3: The Palestinian Arab people possess the legal right to their homeland and have the right to determine their destiny after achieving the liberation of their country (...).

Article 7: (…) A Palestinian must be prepared for the armed struggle and ready to sacrifice his wealth and his life in order to win back his homeland and bring about its liberation.

Article 8: The phase in their history, through which the Palestinian people are now living, is that of national (*watani*) struggle for the liberation of Palestine. Thus the conflicts among the Palestinian national forces are secondary, and should be ended for the sake of the basic conflict that exists between the forces of Zionism and of imperialism on the one hand, and the Palestinian Arab people on the other. On this basis the Palestinian masses, regardless of whether they are residing in the national homeland or in diaspora (*mahajir*) constitute - both their organizations and the individuals - one national front working for the retrieval of Palestine and its liberation through armed struggle.

Article 9: Armed struggle is the only way to liberate Palestine. This it is the overall strategy, not merely a tactical phase. The Palestinian Arab people assert their absolute determination and firm resolution to continue their armed struggle and to work for an armed popular revolution for the liberation of their country and their return to it (…).

Article 15: The liberation of Palestine, from an Arab viewpoint, is a national (*qawmi*) duty and it attempts to repel the Zionist and imperialist aggression against the Arab homeland, and aims at the elimination of Zionism in Palestine. Absolute responsibility for this falls upon the Arab nation - peoples and governments - with the Arab people of Palestine in the vanguard. Accordingly, the Arab nation must mobilize all its military, human, moral, and spiritual capabilities to participate actively with the Palestinian people in the liberation of Palestine. It must, particularly in the phase of the armed Palestinian revolution, offer and furnish the Palestinian people with all possible help, and material and human support, and make available to them the means and opportunities that will enable them to continue to carry out their leading role in the armed revolution, until they liberate their homeland.

Article 19: The partition of Palestine in 1947 and the establishment of the State of Israel are entirely illegal, regardless of the passage of time, because they were contrary to the will of the Palestinian people and to their natural right in their homeland, and inconsistent with the principles embodied in the Charter of the United Nations; particularly the right to self-determination.

Article 20: The Balfour Declaration, the Mandate for Palestine, and everything that has been based upon them, are deemed null and void. Claims of historical or religious ties of Jews with Palestine are incompatible with the facts of history and the true conception of what constitutes statehood. Judaism, being a religion, is not an independent nationality. Nor do Jews constitute a single nation with an identity of its own; they are citizens of the states to which they belong.

Article 22: Zionism is a political movement organically associated with international imperialism and antagonistic to all action for liberation and to progressive movements in the world. It is racist and fanatic in its nature, aggressive, expansionist, and colonial in its aims, and fascist in its methods. Israel is the instrument of the Zionist movement, and geographical base for world imperialism placed strategically in the midst of the Arab homeland to combat the hopes of the Arab nation for liberation, unity, and progress. Israel is a constant source of threat vis-à-vis peace in the Middle East and the whole world. Since the liberation of Palestine will destroy the Zionist and imperialist presence and will contribute to the establishment of peace in the Middle East, the Palestinian people look for the support of all the progressive and peaceful forces and urge them all, irrespective of their affiliations and beliefs, to offer the Palestinian people all aid and support in their just struggle for the liberation of their homeland.

Article 26: The Palestine Liberation Organization, representative of the Palestinian revolutionary forces, is responsible for the Palestinian Arab people's movement in its struggle – to retrieve its homeland, liberate and return to it and exercise the right to self-determination in it – in all military, political, and financial fields and also for whatever may be required by the Palestine case on the inter-Arab and international levels.

Article 29: The Palestinian people possess the fundamental and genuine legal right to liberate and retrieve their homeland. The Palestinian people determine their attitude toward all states and forces on the basis of the stands they adopt vis-à-vis to the Palestinian revolution to fulfil the aims of the Palestinian people.

5

BLOUDAN ENDORSED BY ACADEMICS

In line with the proposals of the spiritual and political leaders at the pan-Arab international conference in Bloudan (Syria) in 1937, the wars of destruction waged by Arab leaders in 1948, and the 1968 appeal by the PLO, in 1968 around four hundred Muslim scholars at the Sorbonne called on Muslims worldwide to wipe Israel off the map. Once again it was stated that Israel has no right to exist. This was the Fourth Conference of the Academy of Islamic Research, which was founded in June 1961 by the National Assembly of the United Arab Republic. The first three conferences were held in March 1964, in May and June 1965 and in October 1966. The Academy acts as a scientific institution of Al-Azhar University in Cairo and has 50 Egyptian members and 20 members from the surrounding countries. All are chosen by the President of the Republic. During almost all nominations there is considerable debate about the constitution of the Palestine Liberation Organization, in which it is repeatedly stated – almost like a chorus – that Israel has no right to exist. In the Proceedings of the conference it was specified, down to the smallest detail, that Israel must be destroyed. From Cairo, these Proceedings were distributed all over the Islamic world, as far as distant Malaysia, Indonesia and among Muslims in African countries and in Europe (especially the UK).

At the end of the conference, the participants issued a statement. 'The aggression of the Israelis, which manifested itself when they attacked the territories of Arabs and Muslims and violated that which is most sacred in Islam, namely the sanctuaries and the rites that there take place, quite justifies jihad against them, such as is prescribed by the Holy Koran. For all these reasons, it is the duty of every Muslim – no matter where he lives – to take part in this holy war against the aggressor with its own capabilities and resources. Muslims around the world must not for one moment forget their religious duty to liberate Jerusalem and the occupied country (Palestine). The participants at the conference of scholars call for a reinforcement of the Palestinian people in every possible way in their fight against the aggressor, so that even fiercer resistance can be given. The ulema issue an urgent appeal to Muslims to accelerate the mobilisation of their spiritual forces, i.e. a better education in Islamic values in schools, in institutions and universities, in mosques and in the army, and finally in the media in the broadest sense of the word. They also appeal to all Muslim governments to sever all relations with Israel, because cooperation with the enemy in any form is a violation of the teachings of Islam. The participants at the conference of scholars finally declare that Muslims must not remain bystanders when they see how the racist Zionists act in the Arab and Islamic world and that they should not hesitate to give their lives in defence of their land and shrines: it is a question of reconquering the country that was unlawfully seized (by the Zionists).'

For the conference participants, peace with the State of Israel, or any form of compromise, was quite unthinkable. In any case, they would invariably only interpret every concession as a step towards the ultimate solution: the dissolution of the State of Israel, the return of Palestine to its rightful owners, the Palestinian Muslims, and the departure of the invaders, the Jews. The three-part Proceedings of the Fourth Conference permit no misunderstanding about this.

6

IT STARTS WITH TEXTBOOKS

In the outstanding academic work *Deception: Betraying the Peace Process* by Itamar Marcus and Nan Jacques Zilberdik, we can read how in many textbooks the Palestinian Authority teaches hundreds of thousands of children and adolescents in the West Bank that the State of Israel has no right to exist and should be wiped off the map. In the latest textbooks, which were published in December 2006, the Palestinian Authority has included a large number of maps on which Israel no longer appears. Far from being an exception, this has become the rule in education.

An investigation into textbooks in the Palestinian territories, which was carried out in 1999 by a group of experts in Arabic, yielded the following disappointing results. They examined 140 textbooks that are used in schools in the Palestinian territories and which had been officially approved by the Ministry of Education of the Palestinian Authority. The examined textbooks are used in all public education classes and cover all the subjects that are taught there: civics, grammar, literature, history, geography and Islamic subjects. The researchers selected excerpts in which a typical characterisation is given of Israel: Jews, Judaism and Zionism. They based their investigation around the following questions: Can we say that the image that the textbooks give to Palestinian children of Israel, the Jews and Judaism, represents a positive contribution to the rapprochement between Palestinians and Jews? Should we not expect the Palestinian Authority, based on the Oslo Accords and the Wye River Memorandum, to ensure that the textbooks used in schools gives an accurate picture of Israel and the Jews? Can we not assume, after the Oslo Accords, that in this regard the textbooks of the Palestinian Authority will differ from those in Iraq, Iran, Syria, Egypt and Saudi Arabia, in which an extremely negative view of Israel and the Jews is given in text and images?

The message conveyed in the textbooks of the Palestinian Authority is clearly and explicitly formulated and requires no further explanation: Israel and the Jews are the sworn enemies of the Palestinians, of all Arabs, of Islam, and therefore of all humanity.[1]

All Muslims must commit themselves unconditionally to holy war (jihad) against the conquerors of the Arab land (Palestine). According to the explanations given throughout the examined textbooks of the Palestinian Authority, Egypt, Syria, Lebanon, Jordan, Iran and Saudi Arabia, Jihad means that every Muslim must be prepared to kill and be killed, sacrificing life and limb, as well as his own possessions, for the cause of Allah, in the profound consciousness that anyone who is killed while fighting for Islam will be rewarded in paradise. Throughout the Arab world, the aforementioned textbooks almost make it appear that it is an immutable law that Israel must ultimately be destroyed.

---

1   That the Jews are the enemies of all mankind is a constantly recurring theme in European literature, from classical antiquity to the Third Reich, yet for centuries was absent from Islamic literature. Once again European influences have made themselves felt since the creation of the State of Israel in 1948.

The reward for a slain jihadi consists of fame, endless orgasmic pleasure with a host of virgins, and a blissful stupor produced by endless quantities of alcoholic drinks, which are prohibited for Muslims on earth. The television stations controlled by the Palestinian Authority regularly broadcast films in which children celebrate martyrdom and other children are called on to take up the role of suicide bomber. For instance, Palestinian television showed a downright shocking program, a talk show in which children of the suicide bomber Rim al-Riyashi were asked how many Jews mummy had blown up in the attack. The aim of the interview was to have the children sing the praises of their mother, who ripped five Israelis to pieces in a suicide attack with a bomb belt. Mummy killed five Jews and is now in paradise. In addition to targeted questions about their mummy's heroic deed, the grinning presenter also asks the children to recite a poem about the glory of their mother. The rhyme is all about guns and bombs. The video can be seen at http://www.memritv.org.

This video is a striking example of how over the past few decades, in countless television programs, the Palestinian Authority has brought up Palestinian children to believe that Israel has no right to exist. See, for example, the children's program of 23 February 2013, which is regularly repeated on Palestinian state television. Female presenter: 'And, of course, we will never forget that we have a country that was occupied in 1948 (the founding of the State of Israel), and which own one will be ours again. Think about it, kids. Also remember to honour our traditions, our national sports, traditions of all kinds, our clothes and our food, and everything that makes up the Palestinian tradition: we must protect that. If we don't do that, then the occupation will steal that from us too, in the same way they've stolen our country from us. That's true, isn't it? You agree with me? Bravo!'

7

THE IMAM'S SERMON

During the Fourth Conference of the Academy of Islamic Research (1968), no members of Hamas, Hezbollah, Islamic Jihad or Fatah's al-Aqsa Martyrs' Brigades were invited to speak, but rather the cream of the academics and religious leaders of all the Arab countries. Twenty years later, the views of the Islamic academics, philosophers and theologians had not changed with respect to the State of Israel. In his book *The Crisis of Islam: Holy War and Unholy Terror* (2003), Bernard Lewis wrote: 'No Muslim would ever cede territory that had once been added to the realm of Islam.'

When, during the First Intifada in 1991, hundreds of religious leaders met in Tehran to support the struggle of the Palestinians against Israel, it emerged quite clearly from the presentations that were given that their views on the State of Israel had remained exactly the same as those that had been proclaimed in Cairo in 1968: the State of Israel must disappear. To support the Second Intifada of the Palestinian people, another conference was convened in Tehran on 23 to 25 April 2001. It was attended by more than five hundred representatives from Arab and Muslim countries (academics, spiritual and political leaders). In his opening speech, the Iranian Grand Ayatollah Ali Khamenei denounced Zionism and the State of Israel with unprecedented ferocity. The leader Hezbollah, Sheikh Hassan Nasrallah, issued a warning to the Jews in Israel at the end of his speech in Tehran: 'The

Zionists should now just pack their bags and return to the countries they came from.'

In a closing statement, the religious leaders of the Palestinian Authority called for the Intifada to be continued, because the State of Israel cannot be fought in any other way. 'Abd al-Wahhab al-Masiri, the Egyptian expert in Jewish Studies, said in Cairo in January 2001 that the Palestinians must continue the holy war against Israel, because that would undoubtedly represent 'the beginning of the end of the Zionist entity'. (Many religious leaders never talk about 'Israel', because according to them Israel does not exist!). According to them, the end of the Zionist entity will be determined not only by its colonialist nature, but also by the fact that they cannot defend themselves and cannot continue to count on the support of the West, which is barely able to ensure its own safety. On 21 September 2001, Muhammad Ibrahim al-Mahdi predicted in a sermon in the mosque that 'the war in the Middle East between Muslims and Jews is about to escalate to its ultimate conclusion: we shall invade Jerusalem as conquerors and exile the Jews. (…) We shall establish an Islamic caliphate with Jerusalem as its capital.' The same Al-Mahdi, an official of the Palestinian Authority, sees the Jews in the Middle East not only as a serious threat to the region but also to the entire world. The holy war against the Jews in Israel is the only way for humanity to survive. Azzam Tamini asserted in an interview in an Israeli weekly that the State of Israel will surely disappear in the short term, and will be replaced by an Islamic state, where Christians and Jews, as minorities, will be subject to Muslim authority. However, he welcomed any Jew who would like to live in an Islamic state in Palestine as a dhimmi, as in previous centuries.

When I was preparing the manuscript that was published in book form in 2006, I read dozens of sermons by prominent imams from the Middle East, which had been given in mosques on Friday mornings from 2000 to 2004 and which had generally also been broadcast on television, as well as many articles by journalists. The Israeli journalist Amira Hass, who for many years has shared the daily life of the Palestinians, writes about the immense influence that the imams have on the population with their weekly sermons. When I compare the contents of these sermons and articles with the aforementioned Proceedings of the Islamic Conference which was held in Cairo from 27 September to 24 October 1968 at Al-Azhar University, we again read that the State of Israel has no right to exist and should therefore disappear unconditionally from the earth. As well as Bernard Lewis and Robert Wistrich, Esti Vebman, an expert in the history of anti-Semitism in the Middle East at the Institute for the Study of Anti-Semitism and Racism at the University of Tel Aviv, also comes to the conclusion that it is extraordinarily worrying that such an incredibly wide circle of academics throughout the Middle East should hold the most profound conviction that Israel has no right to exist and that every trace of its existence must irrevocably be erased.

For more than ten years, Vebman studied the articles that were written about Jews in newspapers, weeklies and monthlies in the occupied territories. He concludes that there has been no change whatsoever in the image of the Jews among the Muslims in the Middle East after the Oslo Accords. Jews are constantly described as enemies of Islam, locusts, wild animals, swindlers, traitors, conspirators, thieves, warmongers, cheats and gluttons. Palestine will have to be cleansed of every Jew as soon as possible.

8

A COLONIAL QUESTION

Between 2010 and 2015, Itamar Marcus, founder and director of *Palestinian Media Watch*, and his colleague Barbara Crook, published *A Documentation*. This barely received any attention In the European or American media. On my desk there is a copy of the documentation, of which I read every page with increasing amazement. The book contains more than seven hundred bulletins, published mainly in *Al-Hayat al-Jadida*, the official newspaper of the Palestinian Authority. These explain to the reader, in endless variations, why Israel has no right to exist and why no maps on which Israel appears can be found in the thousands of school textbooks. A central theme in these bulletins is that the Jewish people in the Middle East have never been in any way connected with the country of Palestine. As a constant refrain, we read that Israel was founded by colonial powers. Hitler and his followers had worked out the plan in detail: all the countries of Europe would be cleansed of Jews, who would then be exiled to Palestine, where at a suitable time they could be eliminated more easily than elsewhere. I read the following in the *Al-Hayat al-Jadida* of 6 December 1998: 'The difference between Hitler and Balfour (the British Foreign Secretary) was simple: Hitler had no colonies to send the Jews to. Therefore, he eliminated them. Balfour made Palestine a British colony so that he could send the Jews there. We might say that Balfour is Hitler with colonies, while Hitler is Balfour without colonies. They both wanted the same thing:

to destroy the Jews. Zionism was always central to defending the West against the Jews. Every Jew had to disappear from Europe!'

Why are politicians and religious leaders in Europe and the United States silent about the fact that hundreds of leading Arab scholars and religious leaders have endorsed the four no's of political leaders at their conferences and continue to do so to this day? Why do the aforesaid political and religious leaders say nothing about the broad agreement that exists between Palestinian academics, professors, teachers, politicians, imams, jurists, journalists, columnists, cartoonists and creators of radio and television programs, in terms of the State of Israel's eventual disappearance ? And why do political and religious leaders in Europe and the United States remain silent about the fact that the Palestinian Authority, completely contrary to the Oslo Accords, has still not deleted one iota from the so-called charters, as was clearly agreed, in which ever since the founding of the State of Israel in 1948 it has been formulated in countless variants that the State of Israel has absolutely no right to exist and must be destroyed? Finally, why are political and religious leaders worldwide (with the exception of Hillary Clinton!) silent on the Palestinian education system of Mahmoud Abbas, in which more than one million Palestinian children, pupils and students are taught even today that Israel must ultimately be destroyed in a holy war?

2

Why does Israel not have the right to exist in the Middle East?

In 1974, Golda Meir wrote in her autobiography *My Life*: 'I have never doubted for an instant that the true aim of the Arab states has always been, and still is, the total destruction of the State of Israel, or that even if we had gone back far beyond the 1967 lines to some miniature enclave, they would not still have tried to eradicate it and us.'

More than thirty years later, not much has changed. On 26 October 2005 Mahmoud Ahmadinejad, President of Iran, said: 'The State of Israel must not only be destroyed, but will also be wiped off the map!' Since then he has repeated this numerous times.

Why is the belief that Israel ultimately has no right to exist and should be wiped off the map so widespread among Muslims (academics, professors, teachers, politicians, imams, jurists, journalists, columnists, cartoonists and creators of radio and television programs) in the Middle East? Why was there deafening silence throughout the Arab world in the Middle East about the speeches of Ahmadinejad? Because he neatly voiced the consensus of Islamic scholars, politicians and numerous religious leaders in the Middle East, for whom Israel has no right to exist and therefore must ultimately be destroyed. It is a naive misconception on the part of European and American politicians to think that this is only the goal of terrorist groups such as Hezbollah and Hamas.

1
HUMILIATED BY THE VICTORIOUS JEW

The victorious Jew who founded a state is impossible to reconcile with the traditional image of the powerless Jew who has to live in misery and humiliation.

The reaction of Muslim politicians and Muslim diplomats from the Middle East immediately after the Six-Day War in 1968 is typical. After the war, which went so ignominiously for the Arab peoples, Arab foreign ministers and ambassadors spent weeks involved in discussions in New York with the Foreign Minister of the Soviet Union on decisions to be taken by the United Nations Security Council. One of the Arab ambassadors later reported on these consultations: 'We Arabs called the Six-Day War a setback. (…) The Foreign Minister of the Soviet Union kept intervening to correct us, saying: "No, this was not a setback, you Arabs have suffered a defeat. You have no alternative but to recognise that."' The Arab ambassador reported: 'But we, the governments of the defeated countries in the Middle East, did not want to do that. No, I'm saying it wrong – we simply could not accept these facts.'

And these historical facts are still not accepted by Muslim politicians. The political developments in the Middle East from 1948 to today, in which the Jews were victorious (and continue to be so), are difficult, even impossible, to reconcile with the traditional image of the powerless Jews. In Islamic literature they have for centuries been portrayed as enemies, as cowards (who, according to the Muslims, neither could not would bear arms!), as braggarts and even as whores. But in no way did they constitute a threat to Islam. The appearance of the Zionist Jew in the Middle East, who as a member of the Jewish people wanted to establish a state and, inspired by a nationalist ideology, actually proclaimed that state in 1948, then in the war of independence from 1947 to 1948 secured a military victory over his age-old protectors and tolerant masters (at least tolerant in comparison to the status of the Jews in Christian Europe!), these events could only evoke deep feelings of resentment among Muslims in the Middle East.

The Israeli historian Robert Wistrich writes: 'The Muslims in the Middle East have experienced it as an intolerable affront to their pride that a people of dhimmis, who for centuries were subject to Islamic authority, have succeeded in establishing a sovereign state in the heart of the Arab world. For this reason, the Arab countries conducted the first holy war in 1948 to prevent the establishment of the State of Israel. The injury to their pride was reinforced when they not only lost this war, and then four more times unsuccessfully went to war against the Israelis, but also because as a result of these wars the State of Israel was able to annex even more Palestinian territories.'

The realisation of the Zionist project, the foundation of the State of Israel in 1948 (which before the Second World War had been considered by the majority of European Jews to be a utopian dream), enabled the Jews throughout the Middle East to leave their 'dhimmi status' (legally protected but second-class citizens) a long way behind and to confirm their independence. But, at the same time, the achievement of this Zionist project also aroused deep feelings of humiliation among the former protectors of the Jews. The Arab Muslims, a proud and dominant group of people, were deeply shocked merely by the fact that the protected minority in the Middle East no longer wanted to accept their status below the condescending, semi-loathing, semi-tolerant gaze of their rulers. The Muslims blame the Jews for forgetting their place in Islamic society. This unexpected metamorphosis of the abject, powerless, humiliated and subjected Jew into a Zionist who obtains military victories and therefore is perceived as a threat to Muslim society, has caused a theological, sociological, economic and political fracture in the centuries-old tradition of Islam, which cannot be tolerated. This reprehensible myth of the Zionist Jew is reinforced on a daily basis by feelings of outrage and anger about the robbery, looting and occupation of the Arab Holy Land (Palestine) by Israel. Even today, this metamorphosis of the Jew is experienced as a constant provocation and a scandal. It fundamentally distorts the social, political and religious order in the Middle East, because, in the structure of society, it throws the superiority of Islam into doubt. The hierarchy of relationships between Muslims and Jews in the Middle East has been overturned. On 25 April 1972, the birthday of the Prophet Muhammad, the late President Sadat of Egypt reacted with amazement to this disorder that the Israelis had caused across the Middle East: 'We will not only liberate our land, we shall also eradicate that Israeli arrogance, so that the Jews return to the status they used to have in the Middle East under us. For our book, the Koran, indicates that status quite clearly: "Their destiny is that they shall live in humiliation and misery".'

Muslims in the Middle East interpret the attitude of the Jews, who had previously been tolerated by Islam, as an enormous arrogance that shocks them and affects their faith.

Zionists have violated the order decreed by God. Therefore, only one solution is acceptable: the Jews must resume their old traditional status. The state of disorder that the Zionists have created is seen by Muslims as an impurity, a defilement, a contamination of all of Islamic society in the Middle East. The new situation that has arisen is dangerous, because nothing is in its rightful place and the impurity is contagious. More and more land will be annexed by the Zionists. The State of Israel is a cancer that must be cut out if the Muslims in the Middle East want to survive.

The Algerian politician Ahmed Ben Bella said in an interview: 'The Arabs will never accept the Zionist entity. The Arab people, the Arab genius will never tolerate the Zionist state. If we were to accept the Zionist, that would imply that we accept the non-Arab. We will always want to remove this foreign body from our region. Israel really is a cancer that has spread in the Arab world. What we want, we, the other Arabs, is that we simply want to be in Palestine. Well, we cannot be there in Palestine if the Zionists are also there. If the Jews are prepared to be satisfied with their previous status as subjects, then we shall not drive them into the sea.' Such reactions by Arab Muslims remind us of traditions in India, where uprisings by representatives of an inferior caste are perceived as being such a radical violation of the structure of society that the entire cosmos is shaken.

The matter-of-fact existence of the State of Israel evokes strong feelings of bewilderment and bitterness, indignation and resentment, dismay and anger among Arab Muslims. This is because the people who have achieved one military victory after another over the Arab Muslims were not adherents of a universal religion (Christianity), nor soldiers of a formidable colonial power (such as the Spain of the Catholic

Kings, the vast British Empire or the mighty, brutal Russia), but they were Jews (...), members of a small and weak nation that has been completely powerless since the year 125 of the Christian era and has been living in servitude and misery, scattered among all the nations of the world. Proud (!) Arab Muslims experience that as a terrible humiliation. I read the following in an article by Sabri Abu'l-Majd (December 1972): 'The proud spirit of the Arab Muslims has successively tolerated the Ottoman and British occupation, because Turkey and Great Britain were large, powerful states with mighty armies. But the proud Arab spirit cannot tolerate the occupation of Palestine by the Jews, that is to say by gangsters who came rushing from the four corners of the world and who know no other law than that of the jungle.'

Even today, Arab (Islamic) heads of state, politicians, imams, university professors and journalists in all forms of media (daily, weekly, and monthly publications, radio and television) in Egypt, Jordan, Syria, Saudi Arabia, in the Gaza Strip, the West Bank and in Lebanon, react to this with deep indignation and outbursts of anger. Despondently, they ask again and again: how in God's name is it possible for the Jews, a small group of people that for centuries Muslims have seen as weak and powerless, contemptible and cowardly – indeed, a group of people that Allah himself had for ever cursed, punished and humiliated – to have inflicted so many defeats the Islamic countries in the Middle East? Now the roles have been reversed: after more than twelve centuries of the Muslims in the Middle East ruling over the powerless and humiliated Jews, now the helpless and contemptible Jews are prevailing over the Muslims (certainly in the occupied territories, but actually throughout the Middle East!). Muslims have been deeply shocked in their religious convictions. They become frustrated and traumatised.

This is also the most profound explanation for the fact that the campaign of hate against the State of Israel did not decrease in Egypt and Jordan after the peace treaty with Israel, but actually escalated, for the fact that the Palestinians have never come up with a peace initiative, and that all the initiatives taken by Israel, the United States, the United Nations, the European Union and Russia (the Oslo Accords, the Road Map and the Geneva Accord) to initiate a peace process have come to nothing.

The victories of the Israelis and the defeats of the Muslims raise numerous sociological, psychological, historical, philosophical and theological questions. If the Jews really are what Muslims have always maintained them to be, namely their arch enemies (but enemies that Allah has brought down and rendered powerless because of their incessant rebellion), how can it be explained that for more than half a century now they have achieved one victory after another over the Arabs in the Middle East?

2

HOLY GROUND

Bernard Lewis said some years ago: 'No Muslim would ever cede territory that had once been added to the realm of Islam.'

Why? In 629 Muhammad concluded the first treaty (called *dhimma*) with the Jews of Khaybar in Medina. Muhammad is reputed to have said after the conquest of the city: 'This land belongs to Allah and his Messenger!' After the death of Muhammad, wars of conquest were fought on three continents (Asia, Africa and Europe) and huge areas were annexed and subjected to a process of Arabisation and Islamisation – in other words, they were colonised. Islam was the greatest colonial power in the history of mankind. We can distinguish two waves of colonisation by the Arabs: the first wave from 640 to 750: all the countries around the Mediterranean Sea were colonised (Palestine in 638); and the second wave from 1021 to 1689: the colonisation by the Turks.

It is a political and legal dogma, rooted in long Islamic tradition, that the land that was annexed by Islam in 638 could be expropriated and that the vanquished (the Jews) became the property of the victors (the Muslims). These, after all, are rights that have been bestowed on the Muslims by Allah himself. There are many legal texts that substantiate this assertion.

To give an example: 'Palestine is called fay, because Allah took this country away from the unbelieving Jews in 638 and returned it to the Muslims. Fundamentally, Allah created this country so that the faithful should serve Him with it. Well, the unbelievers (the Jews) did not serve Allah in Palestine, so he gave the land to the faithful Muslims (Jews have been living illegitimately in Palestine for centuries!).' All four major legal schools (those of the Hanafi, the Maliki, the Shafi'i and the Hanbali) have comprehensively elaborated on the above utterance by Muhammad.

They all developed the thesis (it has almost become a dogma!) of the infallible Ummah, the worldwide Muslim community. They base this on Koran 3, 106: 'You Muslims have, in Palestine in 638, become the best community that was brought forth for the benefit of the people, because you encourage proper behaviour and repel the objectionable, and you believe in God.' Well, it has become a common opinion in Muslim circles in the Middle East, which the Ummah has accepted almost as dogma, that since 638 Palestine has been the inalienable property of the worldwide Muslim community.

In this connection, Andrew Bostom refers to a significant fatwa that is regularly cited to emphasise that Israel has no right to exist and should be wiped off the map. In his fatwa of 5 January 1956, the Grand Mufti of Egypt, Sheikh Hasan Ma'moun, wrote the following: 'Muslims cannot conclude peace with those Jews who have usurped the territory of Palestine and attacked its people and their property in any manner which allows the Jews to continue as a state in that sacred Muslim territory. As the Jews have taken a part of Palestine and there established their non-Islamic government and have also evacuated from that part most of its Muslim inhabitants, then Jihad, to restore the country to its people is the duty of all Muslims, not just those who can undertake it.'

'And since all Islamic countries constitute the abode of every Muslim, the Jihad is imperative for both the Muslims inhabiting the territory attacked, and Muslims everywhere else because even though some sections have not been attacked directly, the attack nevertheless took place on a part of the Muslim territory which is a legitimate residence for any Muslim. Everyone knows that from the early days of Islam to the present day the Jews have been plotting against Islam and Muslims and the Islamic homeland. They do not propose to be content with the attack they made on Palestine and Al-Aqsa Mosque, but they plan for the possession of all Islamic territories from the Nile to the Euphrates.'[2]

Andrew G. Bostom also refers to a fatwa that was published a few days later, on 9 January 1956. He writes the following: 'The fatwa of 9 January was signed by the leading members of the Fatwa Committee of Al-Azhar University (Sunni Islam's Vatican) and the major representatives of all four Sunni Islamic schools of jurisprudence. These rulings elaborated the following key initial point: that all of historical Palestine (modern Jordan, Israel, and the disputed territories of Judea and Samaria, as well as Gaza), having been conquered by jihad, was a permanent possession of the global Muslim Ummah ("fay territory", booty or spoils) to be governed eternally by Islamic law.'[3]

If the conduct of jihad, according to the scriptures, represents the fulfilment on earth of the holy will of Allah, then

---

2 Andrew G. Bostom quotes the fatwa of 5 January 1956 in his essay *The Mufti's Islamic Jew-Hatred* (Washington 213, 55).

3 See 2.

it is the start of an irreversible process of Arabisation and Islamisation of countries that were colonised by Islam, in this case Palestine. This means that any reversal of the jihad (if the subject people, in this case the Jewish people, recaptures the national territory, as happened in 1948 when the State of Israel was founded) is an act of sacrilege, an offence against the sanctity of Allah, and an affront to the holy will of Allah. It means that the holy will of Allah is being ignored, mocked, taunted and insulted, because according to his holy will and holy laws the Arab/Muslim peoples are superior to the inferior Jewish people. The conquest of Palestine, the homeland of the Jewish people, which became an Arab colony in 638 by jihad, condemned the Jewish nation to being a homeless people for all time (on which topic there is a very extensive literature!). The Jewish people then had the choice, when threatened with extinction, of fleeing into exile or of remaining in their homeland Palestine, where they would live in misery and humiliation at the mercy of the whims of their Muslim rulers. The subject Jewish people, deprived of their political rights, were doomed to be utterly powerless! Their language, culture, norms and values were replaced by those of the Arab metropolis; an Arab population moved into the cities, the national identity of the Jewish people was eradicated. All that remained of the Jewish people was a tolerated religion. It is for this reason that Bernard Lewis, the world-renowned expert on Islam, said: 'No Muslim would ever have ceded territory that had once been added to the realm of Islam.'

3

THE CULT OF DEATH

What is the crux of the problem? In Amsterdam in September 2007, the French philosopher Bernard-Henri Lévy, the great advocate of freedom and human dignity in today's world, said: 'The Islamic world needs an aggiornamento, a revolution. And it is true that this revolution will only be achieved if the Islamic texts are read in a truly critical manner, if dogmas are open to discussion. This is the crux of the problem: either the Koran remains untouchable and we are head off towards a catastrophe; or we accept the idea that a text can only live by the grace of commentary, by constant revision. Only then will a new era dawn for Islam. This is what happened with the Jewish law and with the gospels. The actual war between civilisations is being fought between moderate Islam and radical Islam. '

Salim Mansur wrote a moving article on 24 July 2014, in which he clearly explains how so many spiritual and political leaders in the Middle East quite wrongly claim a monopoly on the reading of the Koran. Anyone, for example, who says that a text can only have one meaning has not understood a single syllable of the Book of Revelation. In his article, the author also discussed the most profound text in the Koran (31:27). He writes: 'Across the Arab-Muslim world there is the stultifying absence of what it means to be a "people of the Book," of a culture that progresses through criticism and self-examination. The Koran came to be worshipped by

Muslims instead of being read, examined, reflected upon, contextualised, and discussed openly with the understanding that God's Word is infinite in meaning. The Koran 31:27 states, "If all the trees of the earth were pens and the oceans ink, with many more oceans replenishing them, the colloquy of God would never come to an end." This verse means – almost as a warning for Muslims – that no one Muslim should absurdly claim he has a monopoly over its reading, for that would amount to reducing the majesty of God to the smallness of man. The Koran was, nevertheless, turned by a significant number of Muslims into a weapon by which to kill, maim, destroy, enslave others. In this way, they make the "culture of the Book" impossible and the culture of the Enlightenment disappears. Such Muslims have turned God's Word into a cult of death.'[4]

---

[4] From *Gatestone Institute*, 24 July 2014, by Salim Mansur.